Fidget's Folly

Words by
Stacey Patterson

Illustrations by
Vadim Gorbatov

DEDICATION

For Anne P. S. Price, who has been the enduring spark for Fidget's flame. — SP

To scientists, falconers, artists and all volunteers, whose love and admiration preserve birds of prey. — VG

Fidget's Folly

Text © 2012 by Stacey Patterson

Illustrations © 2012 by Vadim Gorbatov

Printed in Hong Kong

10 9 8 7 6 5 4 3 2 1

Library of Congress Cataloging-in-Publication Data

Patterson, Stacey, 1957–
  Fidget's folly / Stacey Patterson ; illustrated by Vadim Gorbatov.
    pages cm
  Audience: Age 4 to 8.
  ISBN 978-0-87842-594-5 (hardback : alk. paper)
  1. Peregrine falcon—United States—Juvenile literature. 2. Peregrine falcon—Conservation—United States—Juvenile literature. 3. Peregrine falcon—Reintroduction—Juvenile literature. I. Gorbatov, V. A. (Vadim Alekseevich), 1940– illustrator. II. Title.
  QL696.F34P388 2012
  598.9'6—dc23
                                    2012021385

Book Design by
Vadim Gorbatov and Nancy Malick

**Published in cooperation with
The Raptor Education Foundation**
P.O. Box 200400, Denver, CO 80220
www.usaref.org

Mountain Press
PUBLISHING COMPANY
P.O. Box 2399 • Missoula, MT 59806 • 406-728-1900
800-234-5308 • info@mtnpress.com
www.mountain-press.com

ACKNOWLEDGEMENTS

This book would not have been possible without the unflagging support of Bill and Eleanor Knox; they gave Stacey her wings. Her husband, Mark, was the wind beneath them. Special thanks are also due to David Knox, Echo's human counterpart who shared in and endured Stacey's own childhood foibles and follies. Steve Eden provided valuable support, as did Kevin Corwin, Tony Angell, Nancy Malick and Andrei Gorbatov.

When *Fidget's Freedom* was released in 2006, we had already experienced the adventure of a journey to Russia in 2004 to finalize details of that book with illustrator Vadim Gorbatov. Little did we know of the next adventure that was awaiting all of us, when a few months later Vadim flew across the Atlantic to visit the Great American West. Author and illustrator met for the first time, and an incredibly diverse array of generous people introduced Vadim to the Rocky Mountains and the Great Plains. These vast and varied landscapes were his inspiration for the beautiful backgrounds depicted in this book.

Stephen and Libby Bodio hosted Vadim in New Mexico, where he experienced a "real" cowboy bar, sketched scaled quail, and ran Central Asian Tazi hounds in the desert. Tom and Linda Perry of the Bar NI Ranch in southwestern Colorado gave Vadim his first look at America's largest game bird, the wild turkey. In Wyoming's timeless Red Desert, he witnessed, for the first time in his life, a gyrfalcon catch wild quarry: the iconic greater sage grouse. For this portion of his stay, we are forever indebted to Wyoming falconers Sam Crowe and Kristie Brown for their gracious hospitality, splendid navigation, and hot coffee.

Special thanks are also due to several members of the North American Falconers Association (NAFA) and the International Association of Falconry (IAF), in particular, Frank Bond and Bill Johnston. The 2006 NAFA Meet and IAF General Meeting both took place in a joint event in Kearney, Nebraska, and these gentlemen enabled our journey with an international delegation to visit the Archives of Falconry at the Peregrine Fund in Boise, Idaho.

As in any labor of love, a vast array of folks kept things running on time while book production periodically took center stage. First and foremost of these are Marie Bolster and Doug Price, whose decades-long support of REF's educational mission have been crucial. The amazing REF docent staff kept 30 raptors cleaned and fed as we traveled; while volunteerism is not a uniquely American phenomenon, it was one aspect of our culture that Vadim found very inspiring.

Above all, this is a book for young people. Many of us were inspired by books about wildlife that we read as children. It is our hope that Natashka Gorbatova and all the children who read about Fidget feel that "spark ignite." We are grateful to everyone who feels the rush of falcons in their veins.

Peter Reshetniak — *President, Raptor Education Foundation*

Anne P. S. Price — *Curator of Raptors, Raptor Education Foundation*

BEFORE:

Not long ago, a man and a woman stood at the bottom of a cliff. Sweat poured down their faces as they pointed their binoculars towards a box nestled into a cliff. They were watching two young peregrine falcons that were living in the box. These attendants had placed them there and their job was to care for the birds.

The peregrines needed help from the humans. Their species was endangered because of a chemical called DDT that was used to kill insects. But, small birds ate the insects and peregrines ate the small birds. DDT made the shells of the falcon's eggs become thin to the point that the eggs were crushed when the mother birds tried to incubate them.

In just a few short years, the peregrines were all but gone from their historical nesting sites in North America.

But the people who loved peregrine falcons wanted the save them. First they helped ban the use of DDT. Then they bred baby birds in incubators so that the egg shells would not break.

When the birds were five weeks old, their caretakers placed them in "hack boxes" and left food for the birds until they learned to fly and hunt on their own.

No one had ever done this before, but these pioneers were determined to help the falcons.

* * *

In the box, one of the birds that the humans had named Fidget had learned how to fly and escape from predators. She had passed the first test in becoming an independent falcon.

But the next test was to come. Would she be able to learn how to hunt on her own?

Fidget nestled into the corner of her box. Her tummy was warm and full of quail. She was not thinking about hunting – instead, her attention was focused on her brother. . . .

F inally.

Fidget fluffed her feathers as her brother walked to the ledge overlooking the valley, mountains and trees.

Finally, Echo was going to fly.

Fidget remained in her spot at the back of the box. She watched him closely as he took a cautious peek.

Fidget was full of herself. The young peregrine falcon had already flown from the ledge to her favorite branch. Except for a close call with a hunting golden eagle, she had frolicked on her windy playground. The lively currents took her up and down and all around.

Echo's feet clung to the ledge. He lifted his wings and flapped cautiously as his feathers ruffled in the wind.

Fidget sleeked her feathers down tightly against her body. She couldn't wait to join Echo on the breeze.

Echo glanced back towards Fidget.
He tightened his grip.

But Fidget was impatient for Echo to fly!
She charged and pushed him off the ledge.

Echo spiraled and somersaulted through the air.
"Kee, kee, kee," echoed back to Fidget
from below.

Fidget was flabbergasted! This was not like when
SHE played on the currents. She leaned her head far
over the ledge to see where Echo would go.

Finally.

Echo stopped tumbling and spread his wings.
He spotted a rocky shelf on the cliff and flapped
towards it, landing on his belly.

He slowly stood and peered up the wall. His
eyes met hers for a second, then he turned away.

Fidget felt relieved. Somewhat. She was glad that
he was okay, but that was not how it was supposed
to be. Peregrines were masters of the sky. What
happened to her brother?

Fidget lifted her head and scanned the valley. There were lots of interesting little birds to watch. She would think about Echo later.

Fidget focused. One bird stood out from the rest. It was flying awkwardly. Fidget's eyes remained on it as a thought flamed inside her mind but quickly flickered out.

The sun hung low in the sky. It gently set over the hills and bathed the valley in purple, crimson and gold. Fidget yawned and puffed her feathers. She settled in for the night.

But the back of the box was lonely. The shadows on the wall wavered in the moonlight. They made funny shapes. The branches outside the box slithered along the sides. They made funny noises.

Fidget slept fitfully for the rest of the night.

Fidget's eyes flew open. Was it morning yet? She looked around the inside of her box. Where was Echo? She leaped to the ledge and peered down. He wasn't on the rocky shelf.

Fidget left the ledge and coursed the pattern of the river. Her keen eyes searched for her brother as they panned the rugged canyon walls. She continued on her path until darkness closed in.

It was too late to go back to the box.

Fidget found a nook in a cliff and tucked herself in. But she could not get comfortable. She missed the fluttering of leaves against the box. She missed its reassuring walls.

But most of all, she missed Echo.

First light glimmered. Fidget was hungry. For the first time in her life, there was no food to eat. She would have to get back to the box.

The sun brightened the canyon. Fidget headed for home. But the plants, animals and trees did not look right. NOTHING looked right.

"Kak, kak, kak," Fidget cried out mournfully.

"Kak, kak, kak," emptily echoed back.

Fidget's tummy felt hollow as she landed on a new branch. Her wings drooped heavily as she stared vacantly into the still afternoon.

The shadows grew long again. Fidget pulled herself in closely to stay warm against the nip of the night.

Light broke early. Fidget's insides gnawed.

A high pitched whistling noise reached Fidget's ears from afar. She swung her head. A small torpedo shaped bird flew into the canyon. The sun glinted off his brown feathered helmet.

"KAK, KAK, KAK!" thundered and echoed across the canyon.

Fidget bobbed her head in excitement.

"KAK, KAK, KAK!" she bellowed back.

E cho landed beside her. He had something in his foot. It was a little bird. Fidget stepped in for a closer look, but Echo turned his back. He fanned his wings and tail as he leaned over his meal and took a bite.

Fidget felt a spark ignite. If Echo could get his own food, then she could too!

E cho launched himself into the air. Fidget followed.

Things started to look right. Why, she knew that rock. She knew that plant, she knew that animal and she knew that tree!

There was the box! Echo banked off towards a branch as Fidget flew to the delicious meal that was waiting for her. She voraciously gobbled it down.

In the morning, Echo was gone. Fidget knew that he no longer needed the box.

A flock of little birds flew by. One was flying awkwardly. Fidget's eyes remained on it as a thought flickered in her mind, then flamed. As it grew brighter, Fidget launched herself in the air. She climbed in circles until she was a speck in the sky.

F idget focused. She found the little bird.
Without wavering her gaze, she folded her
wings and careened towards the earth.
In seconds, she had the bird in her talons.

S he swooped up to an outcropping to enjoy her meal.

Fidget's eyes deepened with understanding. She was now truly a master of the sky.

Summer's heat turned to chill. The amber leaves were dropping from the trees.

Fidget felt the pull of the south. Many birds were heading that way. One by one, flock by flock, they left her valley. Fidget watched them go. Soon she would join them.

The valley would become another place, another time.

T he dawn rose bright and clear.
The light filled the nooks and the crannies glowed.

Fidget knew that it was time to go. The longing for grasslands and plains thundered through her veins.

Fidget set her course on an ancient avian flyway. She lifted her wings and looked around. All was clear.

Fidget beat her wings to the call of time.

With a last glance at her branch and the box, Fidget left her valley behind.

AFTER

Another summer had passed. Two young peregrine falcons made it through their first hurdles of becoming wild independent beings. They could fly, escape predators and hunt for food on their own.

The hack site attendants' jobs were done. They packed up their clothes, camping equipment, and tents and made the long trek home.

Fidget and Echo followed the little birds to their wintering grounds in Central America.

With luck and skill, they would make the long migration back the following spring.

The hack site attendants would be back as well — with more young peregrines.

BACKGROUND

In 1999, the peregrine falcon was removed from the federal Endangered Species List.

Today there are thousands of peregrines on the wing.

The pioneers prevailed — the peregrine is back.

Publisher's Circle

The Raptor Education Foundation gratefully acknowledges the support of the following individuals and families who gave Fidget wings:

The Amirkhanian-Khrlobian Family

Tony Angell

McKinley Cain

Amelia Rood Jantzen

Maya Abigail John

Annelies Karman

Eleanor Knox

Col William D. Knox, USAF (Ret.)

Kassia Pearl Maciejewski

The Shirley McKown Family

Scott and Debra Mund

Marie Basl Patterson

Bette Phelan

Jim and Sue Phelan

Susan Raymond

Mary Jane Sesto

Beverly Williams

Our Long-Term Supporters and Friends

Robert Berry

Marie Bolster

Laura Chapman

Shelley Doris

ECentral

Tony Head

Helen Johnson

Mark and Kathy Konishi

Karen Kleehammer

Bob and Roxanne Koehler

Susan Raymond

Seven Hills Veterinary Center

Jack Tanner and Fairfield & Woods, P.C.

THF Realty